**W9-BQY-419**

"Sumi-e Self-taught"

By Kohei Aida

JAPAN PUBLICATIONS, INC., TOKYO

Published by
Japan Publications, Inc., Tokyo

Distributed by
Japan Publications Trading Company
1255 Howard St., San Francisco, Calif. 94103
175 Fifth Ave., New York, N.Y. 10010
Central P.O. Box 722, Tokyo

Library of Congress Catalog Card No. 68-31248
© 1968 by Japan Publications, Inc.
All right reserved.

First printing: September 1968

Printed in Japan by Toppan Printing Co., Ltd.

Preface

Sumi-e, one of Japan's ancient arts, though not so widely appreciated and practiced today as it was at its height during the Muromachi Period (1392–1573), nonetheless ranks high in the contemporary art world not only in Japan but also abroad. Many Westerners, progressing from a connoisseur's appreciation of the art, have evinced a desire to learn its techniques, so that they may make their own ink-paintings, based on their own ideas.

Although a number of books about sumi-e are in print in foreign larguages, it is my conclusion—after many years of teaching experience—that none of these is sufficiently detailed to permit the student to master the techniques of the art on his own so that he will be able to see an object with his own eyes and transmute it into a free-hand painting of three-toned ink on absorbent white paper—which is what sumi-e is.

My purpose, therefore, in this book is to give the student all the instruction I believe he will require—on brush control, on the delicate balance of ink and water, and on brush pressure—to achieve the shaded lines of sumi-e. I shall endeavor to explain also the correct sequence of brushstrokes and to instil an appreciation of the necessity for freedom of arm movement so integral to sumi-e.

In view of the large number of people who would like to acquire the essentials of the art—and of the small number of teachers in the world—I believe that a book of this kind is not only desirable but necessary.

I have devoted a number of pages to the question of brush control so that the student will have a clear understanding of the three basic strokes that form the keystone of Japanese ink-painting.

I should like here to express my appreciation to Mrs. Gordon L. McComb and Miss Doris Litscher Gasser for their invaluable assistance, without which I could not have written this book.

August 1968

KOHEI AIDA

5

Contents

History of Sumi-e

The precise date when sumi-e found its way to Japan is uncertain, although the assumption is generally made that this occured during the Kamakura Period (1192–1333) and that the source was the Sogen school of painting in China.

In Japan, the first sumi-e artists were Zen priests. The subjects they chose, therefore, were generally of a religious nature. Then, as Buddhism began to spread throughout the country and to reach the common people, sumi-e also became more popular in nature, and soon secular artists were using sumi to paint those hanging scrolls that we call *kakemono* in Japan. Thus sumi-e became an art of its own, freed from the limitations imposed by its earlier religious associations.

The new style of architecture that developed during the Muromachi Period (1392–1573) introduced two fresh elements: the folding screen (the *byobu*) and the interior sliding door (the *fusuma*), both of which provided suitable backgrounds for sumi-e that had hitherto been unavailable to artists working in this medium.

Sotan (1398–1464) and Sesshu (1420–1506), two of the greatest of the Muromachi painters, along with artists of the Kano school (which began in the mid-fifteenth century), were chiefly responsible for developing the art of sumi painting into the typically Japanese style that is so well-known and so widely practiced today.

Characteristics of Sumi-e

Unlike their European counterparts, who until quite recently tended to use landscape merely as background, Chinese artists have, for a thousand years or more, been painting landscapes as subjects in themselves—subjects that required no "human interest" to make them either worth painting or worth looking at.

One of the most remarkable characteristics of Oriental art is the elimination of light and shade in the realistic, Western sense; depth—in Eastern painting—is expressed by dark and light tones. The aim of Western art, over many centuries, was an ever-more accurate rendering of *chiaroscuro*, of light and shade, which can result only in the capturing of a fleeting moment of time; the aim of eastern art has been the depiction of the timeless vision of the soul—the thing, not as it appears at a given moment, but as it is in its essence. Sumi-e, born out of this desire, partakes of its quality. In some respects, in its simplicity and its avoidance of light and shade, it may be compared to abstract art.

Of the utmost importance in a sumi-e composition is the use of empty space (*yohaku*): it does not just happen; it must be carefully planned to give balance to the composition and impart a sense of dimension.

Above all, sumi-e is an immediate painting: the first form is the final form; there are no preliminary sketches. Light and dark tones must be painted simultaneously—with the same ink and the same brush—and so freely that details lose their importance. A simple, black monochrome painting may suggest numerous colors, but sumi-e may also use colored inks; when it does, it is known as *mokkotsu*. *Suiboku* is the name given to sumi-e done in shades and tones of black-and-white alone. In either case the technique is the same.

The movement of the brush should express the freshness of spring and the freedom of a bird.

How to Lesson

Whether you take a lesson from a teacher, or study the lessons in this book without a teacher, you look first of all at a model painting to be copied. However, you must not attempt to copy the model exactly; if you do, you will be so worried about how you hold the brush that your movements will be stiff; a good picture requires free, relaxed movements. The essence of sumi-e is brush control.

Detail is never sketched in first: at most, perhaps, a very light charcoal suggestion of the general shape. Thus, the finished painting, whether done from memory or from a model, is unique: it is not precisely like any other painting of the same subject, nor is it like the model itself.

Since the basis of sumi-e is brush control, you must practice brush strokes repeatedly, so that eventually you will be able to do your own painting without a model in front of you. The many examples given in this book are useful for learning brush techniques, but once you have learned them, you will sketch your own flowers, landscape, or still life to use as models for your sumi-e.

When doing pencil sketches to serve as models, include as many details as possible, because the purpose of making these preliminary drawings is to become as familiar as possible with the subject. Then, if you can visualize the details when you do the final painting, you will be relaxed and your brush strokes will be easy and sure. When you do a sumi-e from a preliminary sketch, make no attempt to include detail—only try to remember it as you paint. What you are striving for is the essence of the subject, which requires the omission of much inessential detail. You will be an accomplished sumi-e artist when you can at last paint from your own sketch of the actual object.

Focal Point

A sumi-e painting, like all paintings, must have a focal point. If there is more than one focal point, then the main one is that of the most important part of the composition—in other words, the first area you see when you look at a still life or any other composition. All other areas in the painting must be subordinated.

As there are ten objects, for example, in the accompanying picture, the main focal area may be given a value of five; the second, a value of three; and the third, that of two. Two areas in the same composition must never have the same strength; if they do, they clash; and the composition looks weak and unharmonious. In a good composition the varying power of the areas is always evident.

With sumi-e, the sequence of brush strokes from the main focal area to weaker areas is always the same: from the darkest ink or strongest color to succeeding areas as the brush grows lighter. I shall of course explain this point in greater detail as we take up the study of the model paintings.

Materials

You will need to have the following materials before you begin your lessons:

(1) Black ink (*sumi*) in stick-form. There are two varieties of sumi: the Chinese kind (called *toboku*), which is comparatively opaque, and the Japanese (*waboku*), which is transparent. The latter is made from the soot of burned vegetable oil mixed with glue, while *toboku* is a combination of pine wood soot and glue. Both must be kept in a mould for some time before use; the best *waboku* may be kept ten years or more. *Waboku* gives a prettier and clearer color but does not spread so easily as *toboku*. The rubbing end of the ink-stick should be shiny and smooth, and when it is rubbed with water on the ink stone should not make any noise.

(2) Ink stone (*suzuri*). At first sumi-e artists used not only stone but also copper and tile; now most artists use natural stone. *Suzuri* made of synthetic stone are also available and are cheaper than those of natural stone. A good *suzuri* should be neither too soft nor too hard, and the easiest shape to handle is the rectangular one shown in the illustration. The deep end of the *suzuri* is the well or pond, where the ink is stored after being mixed. Mixed ink is good for only one day, after which the color loses its freshness and becomes dull and muddy. The *suzuri* must be thoroughly washed with cold water after every use; hot water should be avoided as it tends to weaken the stone.

(3) Brushes (*fude*). Although brushes intended for painting look exactly the same as writing-brushes, the former are more flexible when wet and so move more easily in all directions. Shown in the illustration, from left to right, are:

(a) *Mokkotsu fude*, the standard sumi-e brush. These may be large, medium, or small, and most of them are made of deer hair in bamboo handles. White deer hair is the softest, but red is the most popular with sumi-e artists. On the basis of his experience, the artist will naturally choose the brush that suits him best.

(b) *Menso fude*, for drawing fine lines. Smaller in diameter than the *mokkotsu fude*, this brush also comes in several sizes. The hair, which is long and strong, may be either red deer or yellow weasel. Regular Japanese painting makes use of other kinds of brushes for color and shading, but for sumi-e the *mokkotsu fude* and the *menso fude* are sufficient—although some sumi-e artists make use of still a third type.

(c) Wider and flatter than the *mokkotsu fude*, this brush may be used in painting distant mountains or snow scenes or in shading in a background. The whole brush must be wet, with one side gray to give the shading or delicate shadow. Of the many sizes available, the most convenient for purposes of shading are the one-and-a-half inch and the three inch.

(4) Paper (*kami*). Two types are most commonly used:

(a) *Toshi* (or Chinese paper). This is a very elegant paper and highly suitable for the freshness of sumi color; it has the further advantage of remaining unchanged for many years. It comes in two shades, white and yellow-tan, and in large sheets, which are cut to the desired size. In recent years, real Chinese *toshi* has become so scarce that *toshi* made in Japan is now in almost universal use.

(b) *Gasenshi*. This very white paper is highly absorbent, so you must be careful, when you use it, of the amount of water on your brush when you start to paint, and you must never stop in midstroke. Considerable practice is needed to handle this paper correctly.

(c) *Gahoshi* and *seihoshi* are two other types of absorbent paper; there are many more of course.

(5) Brush dish (*hissen*). Used for cleaning brushes, the *hissen*, which may be either round or rectangular, is divided into two or three compartments so that the cleaning water is not all dirtied at the same time. Some *hissen* are made of china, some of metal, china being the more popular. Of course any sort of container may be used to clean brushes, provided only that it be totally free of grease or oil.

(6) Plate. A shallow bowl, about six inches in diameter, is necessary for mixing shades of grey and also for fixing the point of the brush; it should be plain white, with no distracting design. In addition, small, three-inch shallow bowls are useful for mixing colors (the set shown in the illustration contains five plates), although more convenient is an ordinary, large water-color palette.

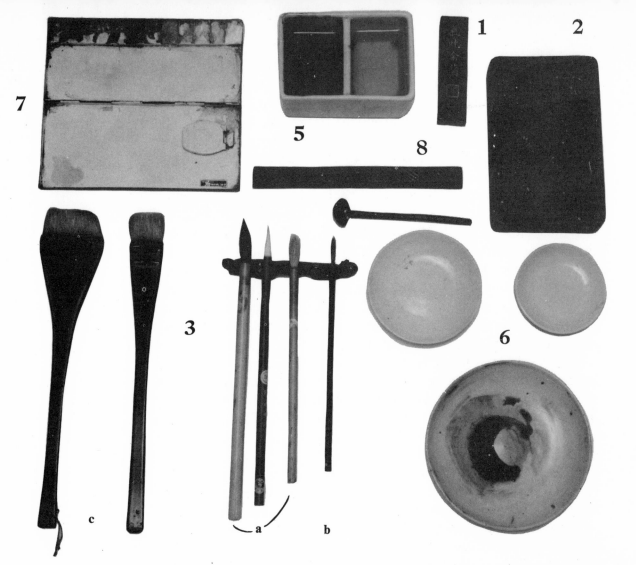

(7) Colors. The sumi-e artist has a choice of two types: colors made either in stick-form, like ordinary black, or in small china compartments. In either case they are made with a glue base which is easily melted in water. In the beginning, sumi-e artists limited their range to a very few colors—blue, red, yellow, brown, and green—but now many artists use ordinary water colors, although they are likely to insist on the real Japanese blue, which is made only in Japan by a process that involves squeezing the juice from *ai* grass, drying it, and then mixing it with glue.

(8) Paper-weight (*bunchin*). Used to hold the paper in place while work is in progress, the *bunchin* is usually made of metal, such as iron or copper, or china; but since iron sometimes chips or stains the paper, it is better to use either china or some chromium plated metal.

The artist must constantly bear one thing in mind when using these materials: they must all be kept free of grease and oil at all times. Should the brush become oily, it will not keep its point after being wetted, and dark and light shading becomes impossible. Wash all sumi-e materials separately from kitchen dishes, and wash the black sumi out of the *suzuri* by hand or with the use of a clean paper towel. Then wrap it in newspaper to protect it from dust and dirt. After use, swish the brush through the water in the *hissen*, then wipe it dry on clean, absorbent paper, make a nice point, and roll it up in a small sheet of any material to protect it. If the brush should become contaminated by oil or grease, wash it carefully in cold water. Hot water should *never* be used, as it ruins the hairs and also melts the glue that holds them in the handle. For this reason, also, the brush should not be left in water for a long period of time. Should the other materials be contaminated, wet some paper and wipe them briskly to free them of all trace of oil or grease; if necessary, a mild cleanser may be used.

Care of Utensils
All brushes and containers should be thoroughly cleaned after every use. Wash brushes in cool water until every trace of ink is gone; the plate you have used for mixing paints, the *suzuri*, and the water container should also be thoroughly cleaned in cool water. Soap should *not* be used since it may leave an oily film or a residue of some sort that might spoil your next painting session. Occasionally, despite all precautions, some such film or residue may appear anyway; in that case, wipe the utensils with a dry cloth or paper towel before you begin to paint.

How to Use *Sumi* Stick and *Suzuri*

The two parts of a *suzuri* are the pond, or well, where the water is kept, and the rest of the stone, called the hill, where the ink-stick is rubbed. The *suzuri* should be placed at your right, with the pond at the top, and the pond should be about three-quarters full of water when you start.

With the rubbing end of the sumi-stick scoop about half a teasponful of water onto the hill; then, holding the stick with three fingers, as shown in the illustration, rub it back and forth in straight strokes about three inches long. Use only moderate pressure and keep the rubbing end of the stick flat against the *suzuri*.

Counting the back and forth motions as one stroke, rub the stick about forty times until the half-teaspoonful of water on the hill becomes sticky and very black. Then push this into the pond, scoop up once again a very small amount of water, and rub the stick another forty times. Push this back into the pond and repeat the cycle five or six times; the pond water becomes darker and darker until at last it is very black.

You must never put the point of the brush directly into the pond—it would pick up too much water and become too black, making shading impossible. There should always be an extremely small amount of prepared ink (about a quarter-teaspoonful) on the hill, and it is here that you moisten your brush. It should not be a "puddle" of ink, only enough to moisten the brush a few times.

When the ink becomes too light, bring a little more water up on the hill and rub the stick back and forth about ten times. If you are doing a large number of pictures, you will have to scoop water up from the pond quite often, rubbing with the ink-stick each time to freshen up the black.

Once the ink has been mixed, it may be used only for one session; it must never be saved for the next day: old sumi, called "sleeping ink," will have lost its shine and the freshness of color that sumi-e demands. Therefore, after you have finished painting, *always* wash the *suzuri;* the next time you paint, begin mixing fresh ink again.

For your ink to be of good consistency, you will have to rub the sumi-stick on the hill of the *suzuri* about four or five minutes. The hill should never be allowed to dry up while you are painting.

Position of Materials and Drawing Posture

As shown in the illustration, the *suzuri* should be on your right, with the big plate below it and the brush dish above. If you use a brush rest, put it on the right of the plate, while the colors may be placed above the paper or to the left of the *suzuri*, whichever you find more convenient. It is useful also to keep a damp cotton cloth in another small plate to absorb excess water from the brush: this permits greater brush control.

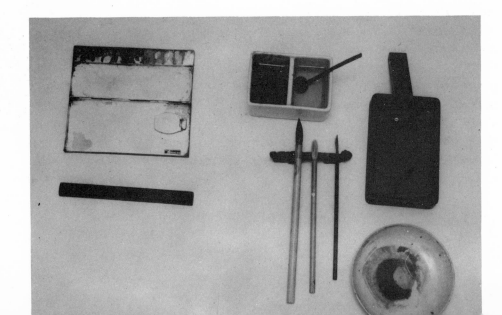

The correct posture for sumi-painting is to sit straight in your chair and to pull it so close to the table that your body almost touches the table's edge. You will find that a dining table is probably a little too high for comfort; if so, put a cushion on the chair that you are using. The optimum distance between eye and paper is seventeen inches: this permits you to have an over-all view of the composition and also prevents your arm from tiring. If you are painting with your right hand, put your left hand on the table, as shown in the illustration, leaning slightly on it so as to steady your body and permit your relaxed right arm to move easily and surely, without any involuntary tremors.

How to Hold the Brush

The brush is held between thumb and forefinger, with the thumb at approximately the mid-point of the handle, which rests against the bend of the second joint, as shown in Illustration A. The brush is held straight up and down for thin lines or outlines.

In Illustration B, the brush is shown tilted toward the painter at an angle of about 45°. This is probably the most commonly used position, but any position intermediate between this and that shown in Illustration A may be used according to the subject. See Diagram 1.

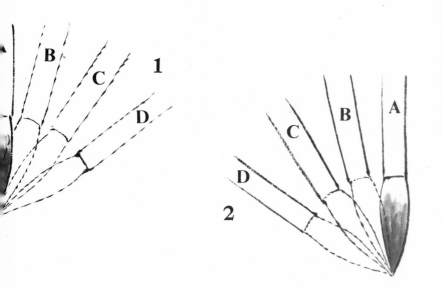

Holding the brush as in Illustration A, bend your wrist so that it tilts away from you (Illustration C). Here again, various positions between straight up-and-down and a forty-five degree angle may be used as needed (Diagram 2).

The brush is *never* held like a pencil, with the handle resting against the fold between the thumb and forefinger, as shown in Illustration D.

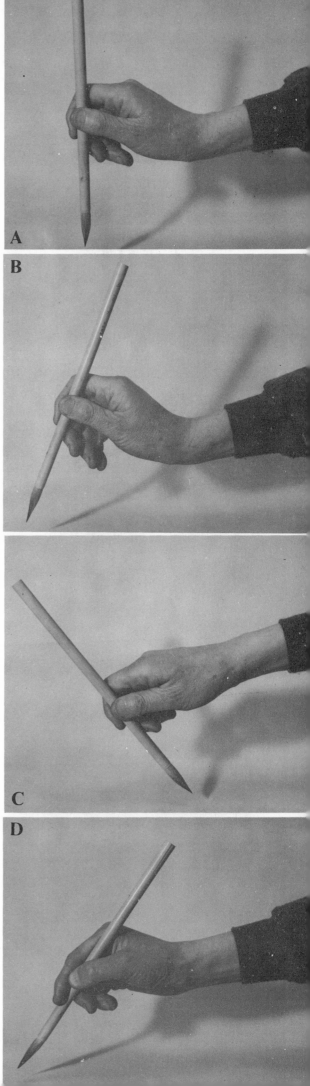

How to Make Dark and Light Tones

One of the three essentials of sumi-e is the ability to make dark and light tones with the same brushstroke, as shown in the accompanying illustration. In the one line, black gradually changes into gray. This technique—of having several tones on the brush at the same time—is the heart and soul of sumi-e; without it, there is no sumi-e; and it is used in large pictures, like screens, as well as in small ones, such as Christmas cards. Some subjects, naturally, require a great deal of black, and others very little, but the technique remains the same. I shall review the details of it again and again.

Set out your materials and freshen your ink by bringing some water up on the hill of the *suzuri*, rubbing the stick back and forth several times. The hill must be neither dry nor too wet, and the ink should be spread evenly over it. As it evaporates, *keep bringing up more ink* and rubbing back and forth six or seven times.

Rest the ink-stick on the far end of the *suzuri*, with the wet point over the pond.

You must master the ability to paint several tones with one brush stroke, as shown above.

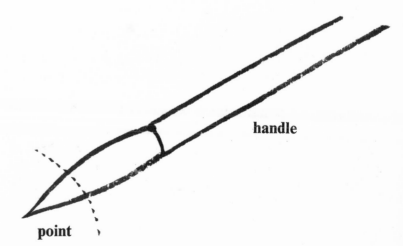

handle

point

16

1. Wet the brush in clear water.

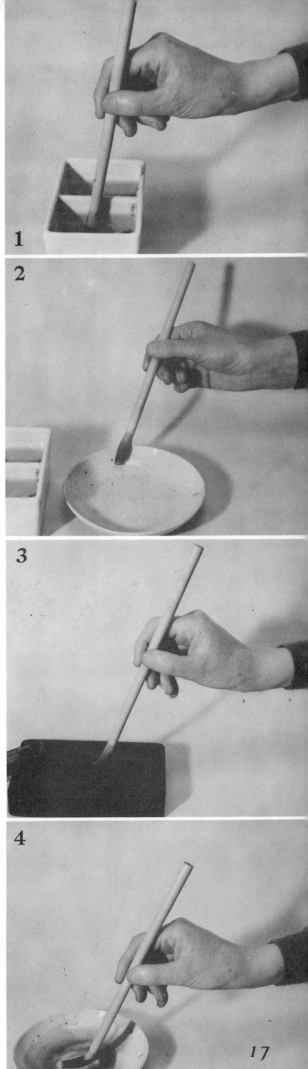

2. Remove excess water in the plate. If the plate is oily or greasy, the ink may separate or the liquid may form droplets. In that case, the plate must be scrubbed dry with a paper towel.

3. Using only about one-third of the tip, pick up some black ink from the hill of the *suzuri* with your brush.

4. Combine the black ink on your brush with the water in the plate to make a gray (*tanboku*) of exactly the same tone as that shown here. When, in the course of painting, you find there is too much liquid in the plate, *it must be partly emptied.*

5 6

5. Pressing the brush flat against the plate, pull it toward you in a wavy line. Repeat twice, to ensure that the hair of the brush is flat. You will now have gray ink about half-way up the tip of the brush; keep the upper half clean.

6. Twist your wrist so that your thumb is now on top, keeping the handle of the brush horizontal and the flattened sides of the tip parallel with the top of the table. Lay the brush against the edge of the plate, allowing about an inch and a half of the handle inside the plate but taking care not to let the tip touch the bottom of the plate.

7
8

7. Using a certain amount of pressure, pull the brush smartly across the edge of the plate to remove excess ink. Repeat three times. The purpose of this operation is to remove excess gray, so that the brush will not be too wet. The hair in the tip of the brush must be kept flat at all times, and the handle and flattened sides of the tip must be parallel with the top of the table.

8. Without turning your hand, rotate the brush between thumb and forefinger so that the flattened side of the tip that was formerly on bottom is now on top.

 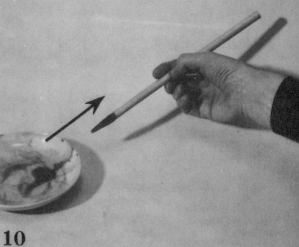

9 10

11

9. Repeat process shown in Illustration 6.

10. Repeat process shown in Illustration 7.

11. Returning brush to its original position between thumb and forefinger, pull it very lightly across the rim of the plate two or three times to straighten the tip, which will have got curved during the process of removing excess ink. If the brush still seems too wet, pull it across the rim of the plate another time or two. There can be no exact rule here, but experience will soon tell you when the brush is too wet.

12

12. To point the tip of the brush, touch it against the edge of the plate. Touch only the very tip. If you attempt to make the point from further back, the point itself will become round and the hair in the tip will remain flat.

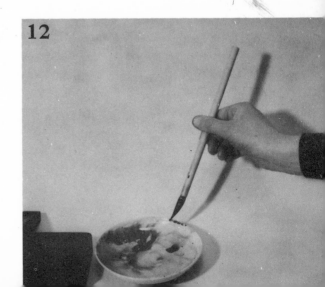

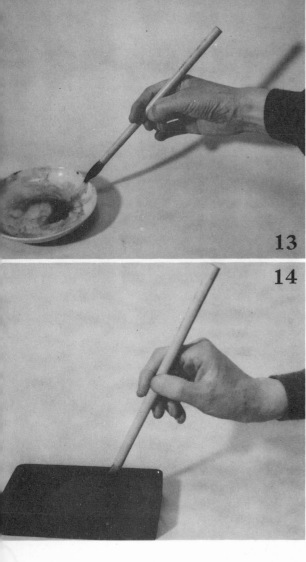

13

14

13. Turn the brush between thumb and forefinger and complete the point on the other side, then rotate the brush back again. The tip should now be flattened and pointed, as shown in the accompanying diagram.

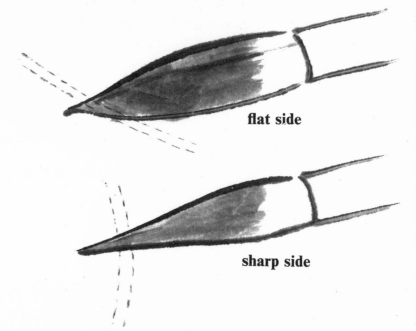

flat side

sharp side

14. Holding the brush at a forty-five degree angle to the *suzuri*, pick up some black ink by making a wavy line across the hill, as shown. The black should not be straight across the tip, nor should the brush be held at an angle less than forty-five degrees. Generally speaking, sufficient pressure is applied to blacken only the first third of the tip, but sometimes—depending on the subject—more or less black may be used.

If you push or pull the brush in straight lines across the hill of the *suzuri*, the point will be broken.

15. After you have as much black as you think suitable on the tip of your brush, you must blend the gray and the black so that the shading will be even. Otherwise you will get too much contrast (as shown in Diagram A); the line you paint should look like that shown in Diagram B. This is accomplished by making a wavy line with your brush on the right side of the plate, keeping the flattend side of the brush against the plate and the black edge down.

The wavy line should resemble that shown in Diagram D, with approximately four or five motions from "a" to "c". This wavy line is then repeated, taking care to keep about two-thirds of the brush gray.

Third, make a wavy line very lightly with the black edge, as shown in Diagram E.

15

A

B

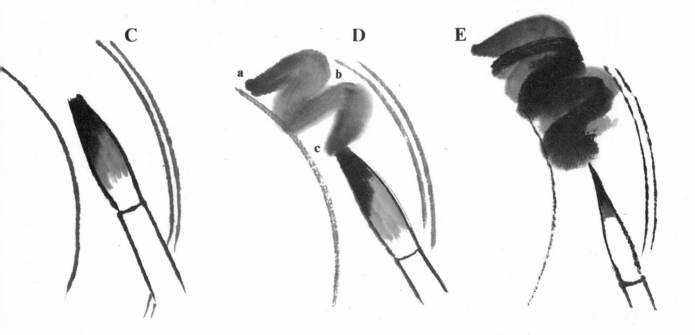

C   **D**   **E**

a   b

c

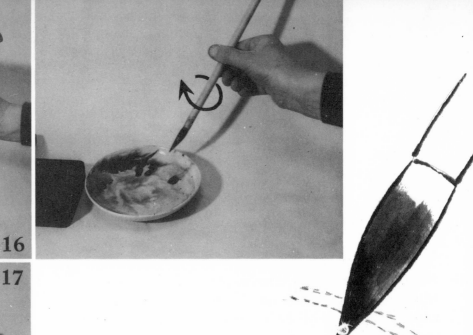

16. You will find that after having made the three wavy lines against the side of the plate, the point of the brush will have become somewhat flattened. Resharpen it by tapping first the dark side, then the light side, against the right (or dry) edge of the plate.

17. During this process, a small amount of gray ink will have fallen down toward the point, so once again a drop of moisture must be removed. This is done against the rim of the plate, keeping the handle of the brush horizontal. Remake the point of your brush by touching first one side of the tip against the rim of the plate, then the other, as shown in Illustrations 12 and 13. Now rotate the brush between thumb and forefinger so that the dark side is on top. The side of the brush that touches the paper must *always* be the light side; the dark side must *always* be on top: this is most important.

18. The whole process of preparing the brush, as I have explained it, ought to take the beginner at most thirty or forty seconds; an experienced painter will find he can do it in about fifteen seconds. For practice, thin calligraphy paper or newspaper is adequate.

22

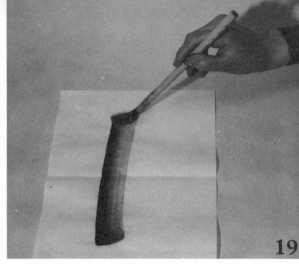

19

20

19. Holding your brush at an angle of 45°, draw a line from left to right, then one from right to left. In both instances, the top of the line must be dark and the bottom light. If the lines are not properly shaded, clean your brush and begin the exercise again. After you have drawn several lines, you will find that your brush is dry, so return to Illustration 5 and repeat the process.

20. When painting, you will often hold your brush in such a way that the handle points away from your body. Here again the light side of the tip must touch the paper. However, when you hold the brush perpendicular to the paper, with the handle pointing neither toward you nor away from you, you paint with the point of the brush and dark and light sides are immaterial. This position is used for painting thin lines, such as, perhaps, the branches of a tree.

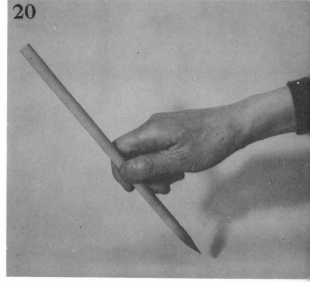

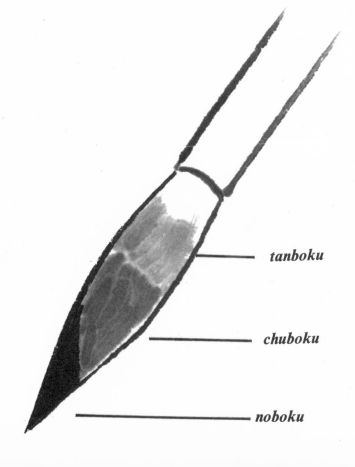

tanboku

chuboku

noboku

Three Basic Strokes

Illustrated here are three basic strokes for painting a bamboo stalk: the straight stroke (A), the side stroke (B), and the half-side stroke (C).

In (A) the brush is held straight up and down, at a right angle to the paper, and is moved straight in that position. Further examples of this stroke are given on page 29.

The side brushstroke (B) is the one most commonly used in sumi-e. Here the brush is held at an oblique angle to the paper, and the line made is a wide one, as shown on page 28.

The brush position in (C) is midway between those of (A) and (B), and the line made is wider than (A) but narrower than (B). Examples of the half-side brushstroke are given on page 29.

A

B

B

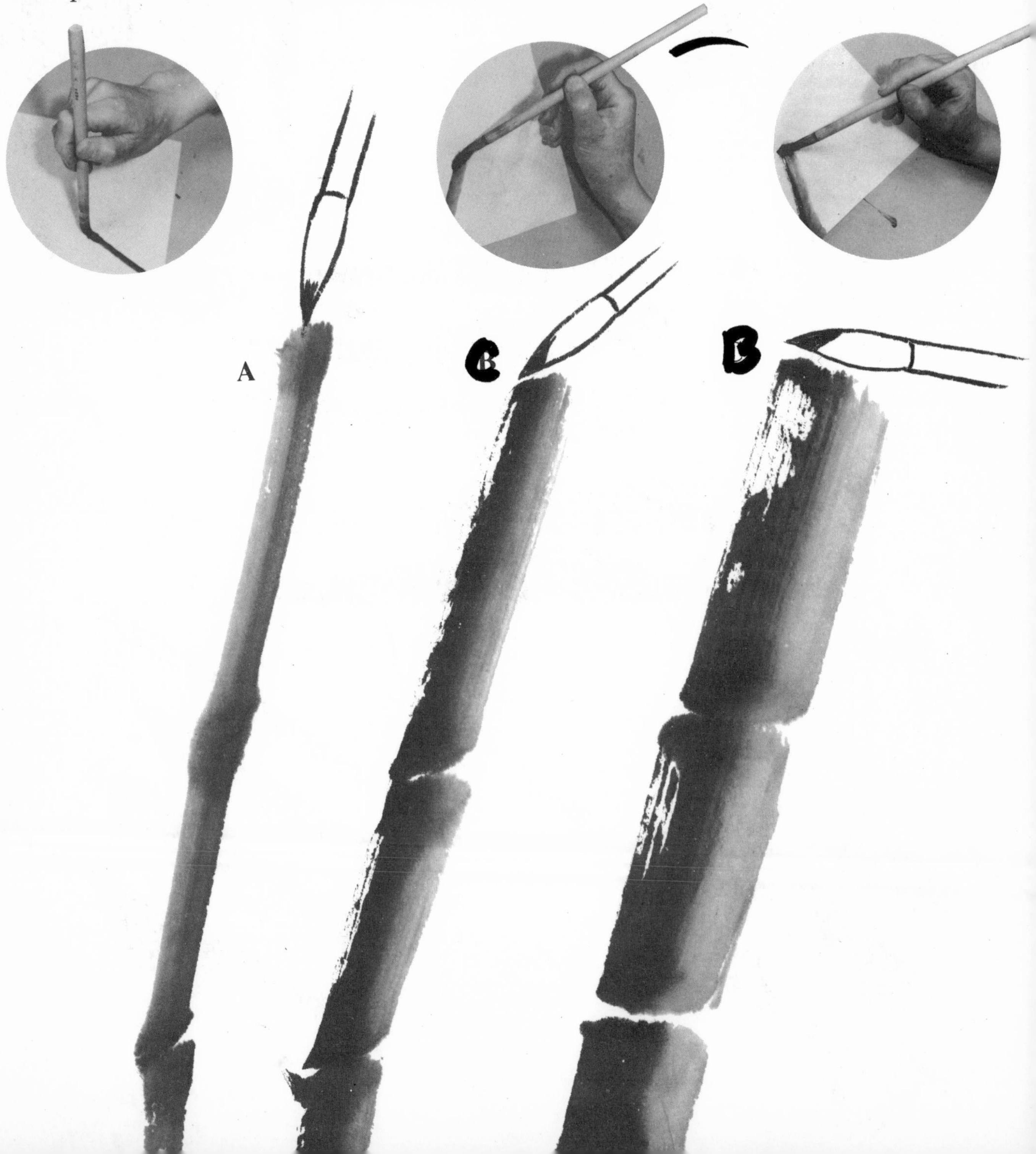

These strokes may be painted in any direction: that is to say, from top to bottom or bottom to top, from right to left or left to right, and so on.

While both (A) and (B) in the accompanying illustrations are side brushstrokes, the movement of (A) begins right on the paper whereas (B) glides down from the air above onto the paper and then back into the air again. (B) is more commonly used in sumi-e than (A).

All the examples given on the pages immediately following were made by using the side brushstroke.

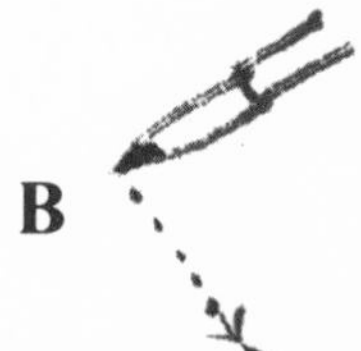

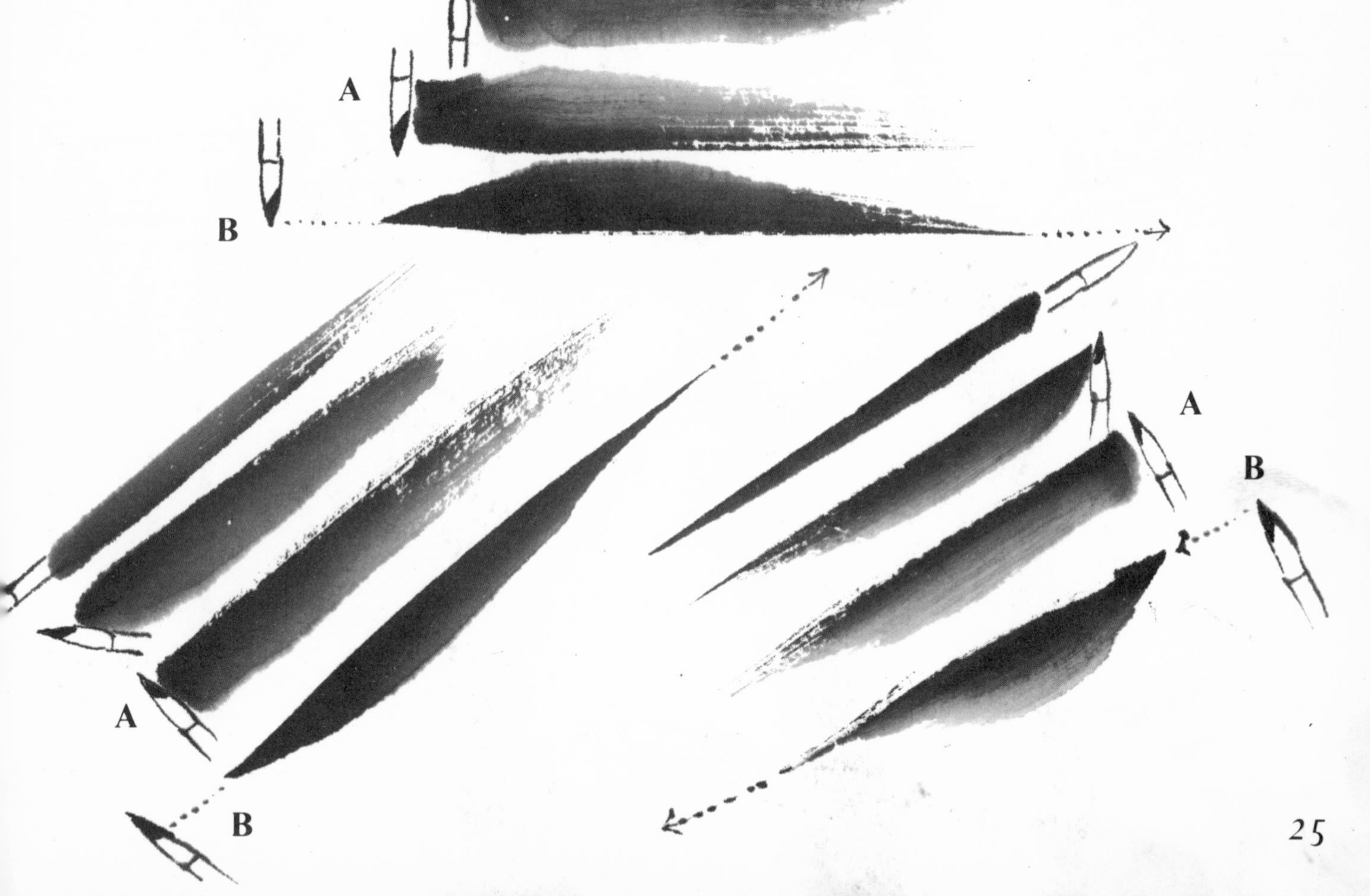

25

Study the hand positions shown in the accompanying drawings. Then hold your hand in the same positions and practice until you achieve the kind of line shown with each of the four positions. Use your whole arm and a full sweeping movement. Keep in mind the comparison with the landing and take-off of an airplane. The line in the lower right hand corner is the result of an uncompleted brushstroke—that is to say, the brush stopped on the paper instead of gliding off into the air.

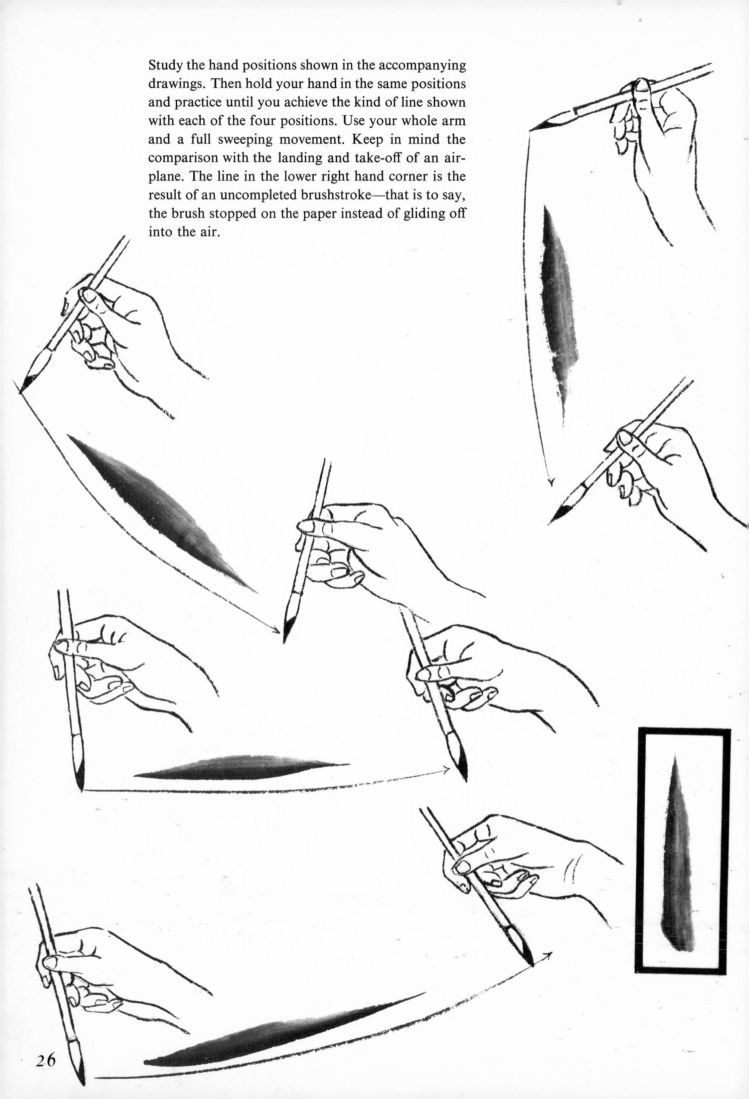

Basic Side-brushstrokes

The accompanying chart shows the correct position of the brush for painting various strokes. These are all side brushstrokes, and the broad side of the brush is used in every case. Practice painting the strokes from the point marked START, moving clockwise around the circle.

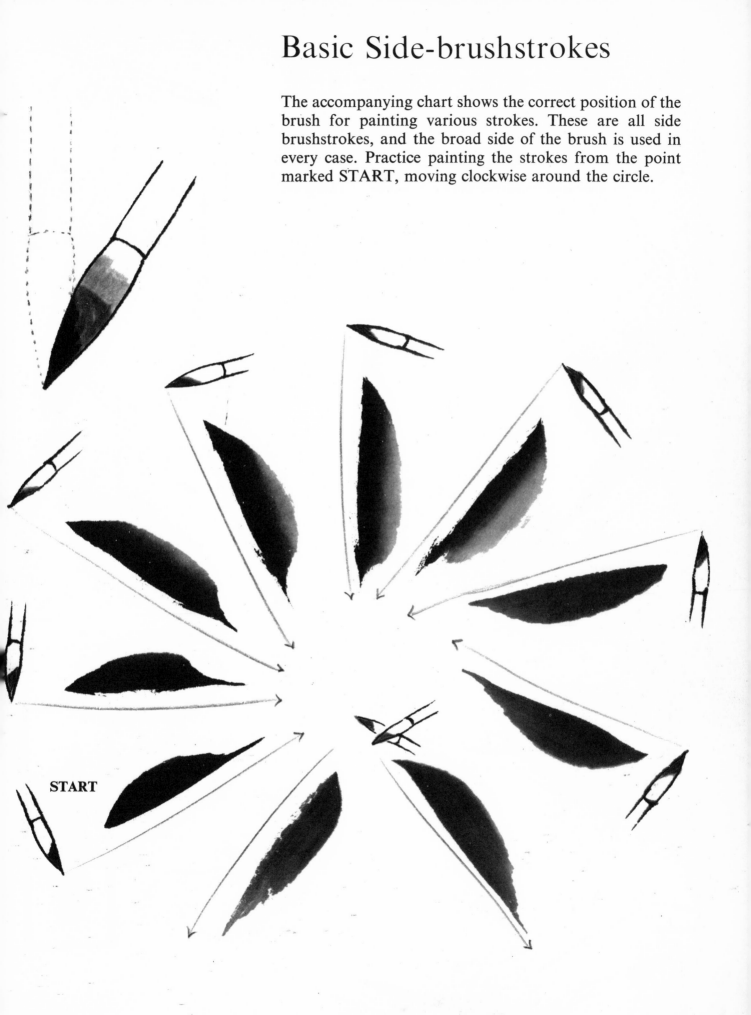

START

Examples of the Three Brushstrokes

Given here are examples of the three brushstrokes.

(A) Side brush

(B) Straight brush

(C) Half-side brush

Painting a Composition

Initial practice will center around four subjects—the orchid, the plum blossom, the bamboo, and the chrysanthemum—in the painting of which all sumi-e brushstrokes are employed. Once you have mastered the strokes involved in these four subjects, you will be ready to create your own compositions—which is, of course, the object of the lessons given in this book.

The Orchid

Leaves

Look first at Illustrations No. 3 through No. 18 (pages 17–22). Then follow the directions for putting three tones—light gray, dark gray, and black—onto your brush. You are now ready to begin practice.

Rest your left hand on the table to prevent your body from moving and to give your right hand more freedom of action.

As you practice, follow the guide-lines: these will tell you the position of the brush and the arrows will indicate the direction of the stroke. When you use a straight up-and-down position, you will find it best to keep the dark side of the brush toward you.

In painting the orchid leaves, the handle of the brush should be tilted slightly away from you: this will ensure that you follow the important rule of touching the light side of the brush to the paper. You paint the leaves, as you will see by the direction of the arrows, from left to right.

Movement should come, not from the wrist, but from the entire arm, and you should hold the brush lightly, so that your strokes will be free and steady, but not too fast.

Start the leaf with a light stroke, press down slightly to broaden the line, then lessen your pressure, then press down again: this will give the leaf a free-moving, rather willowy look. You should feel as though even the slightest breeze might rustle it.

You will note that the first three leaves painted are dark, with little variation in tone. The whole composition, however, should have tones that vary from dark to light, and the leaves should have an interesting arrangement, being neither too close together nor too far apart. They must seem as though they stem from one root.

As you finish the leaf strokes, move your brush gradually off the paper and into the air. When drawing the small strokes, glide smoothly onto the paper and off again, as in the familiar comparison of the landing and taking-off of an airplane.

2

1

5

4

3

7

Flowers

Since the flower of the orchid plant is lighter in tone than the leaves, you must use a drier brush in painting it. Dip the tip of the brush lightly into medium black and, using the zig-zag motion that has already been described, blend black ink and water making the medium gray. Now practice painting the flowers, following the numbers and the direction of the arrows given in the accompanying diagram.

Keep in mind at all times that the motion of the brush involves the entire arm and begins about two inches off the paper and ends only when the brush is back in the air again. The arm should move freely, and the movement should be steady and continuous, flowing without halt.

Petals are painted with the point of the brush, and the stroke to be practiced first is slanted only slightly to the side, not completely, as in the chart given on Page 27. A study of the inset will help you in achieving the correct hand position for these strokes. Once you have mastered them, practice the same strokes with a more slanted brush. Two of these strokes are used in painting the leaves of the rose and the camellia.

33

The Bamboo

Stalk

In painting bamboo, a straight brush is used for the stalk itself and a half-side brush for the joints in the stalk. As for the ink, the stalk is painted in medium light gray and the leaves in black. (In sumi-e, light gray is known as *tanboku*, medium gray as *chuboku*, and black as *noboku*. It is advisable for the student to memorize these terms, as they will be used in future lessons.)

For the bamboo, as for the orchid, first dip your brush in tanboku, then pick up a little chuboku on the tip of the brush. Starting at the bottom of the page, on the left-hand side, make a short upward stroke, as always moving your whole arm. When you near the joint, press the brush down slightly to make the stroke wider and lightly bring the brush off the paper. Then press down with a half-side brush, turn the brush so that it is straight, and move lightly upward toward the next joint, where you repeat the operation that has already been described. You will need to practice turning from the slanted brush position to that of the straight brush so that you can do it effortlessly and evenly. Too long a pause in changing brush positions will result in a rounded stroke rather than in the clean-cut stroke that so well expresses the cool, refreshing lines of the bamboo stalk.

While the ink of the stalk is still wet, use a dry brush to accent the joints with noboku, as shown in the diagram.

To paint the small branches, add a little noboku to the tip of your brush and mix it to make chuboku. Remove as mush water from the brush as you possibly can by pulling both sides against the edge of the saucer. The brush used in painting these small branches should have a hard, sharp point. Follow the arrows upward as shown in the diagram.

Leaves

Before you begin painting the leaves of the bamboo, practice the basic brush-strokes given in the chart on Page 27.

When you begin the actual painting, you must use the same free movement of the arm that you learnt in painting the orchid. With bamboo leaves, you touch your brush to the paper rather heavily, then lighten the pressure, gliding up or down and off, following the accompanying diagram. All strokes are painted with a side brush.

Begin by painting the nearest leaf first, which will also be the largest leaf, then move on to the other leaves, indicated by the arrows in the diagram.

In a young bamboo, the leaves tend to be stiff and upright, while in an older bamboo, with its thicker stalk, the leaves hang downward. Practice painting the leaves of both, as shown in Examples.

To make a more interesting composition, use a combination of both old and young bamboos—a straight brush for the young plant, a half-side brush (which gives a wider stroke) for the old plant. With both, press the brush down slightly harder at the joints.

38

The Plum Blossom

As preparation, dip your brush in tanboku, then tip the brush with noboku, in the usual manner, mixing with the customary zig-zag motion on the hill of the *suzuri*. Then practice once again the basic brush strokes as given in the chart on Page 27.

Using a side brush, paint the plum blossom branch from top to bottom and from right to left, as shown in the accompanying diagram. The main branch is painted not in one stroke but in three, all done with the gliding motion that swoops onto the paper and off again. The ink overlaps at the completion of one stroke and the beginning of another. The technique is the same as that used in the brushstrokes shown in the chart, save that the latter end with a point whereas strokes used to paint the plum branch do not.

Large branches are painted with tanboku and a side brush, smaller ones with chuboku or noboku and a straight brush that is as dry as possible. The same straight brush is used to paint the moss (called *tentai*), which varies, naturally, in size.

In painting the plum blossom flower itself, use a combination of large and small strokes to make the arrangement as interesting as you can. The stroke used in painting the petal must not be too thin, and the stamens should be accented to add further interest to the composition.

Stamens

WRONG: The bud does not form a right angle with the branch.

The brush is held in this position when painting the branch shown above.

41

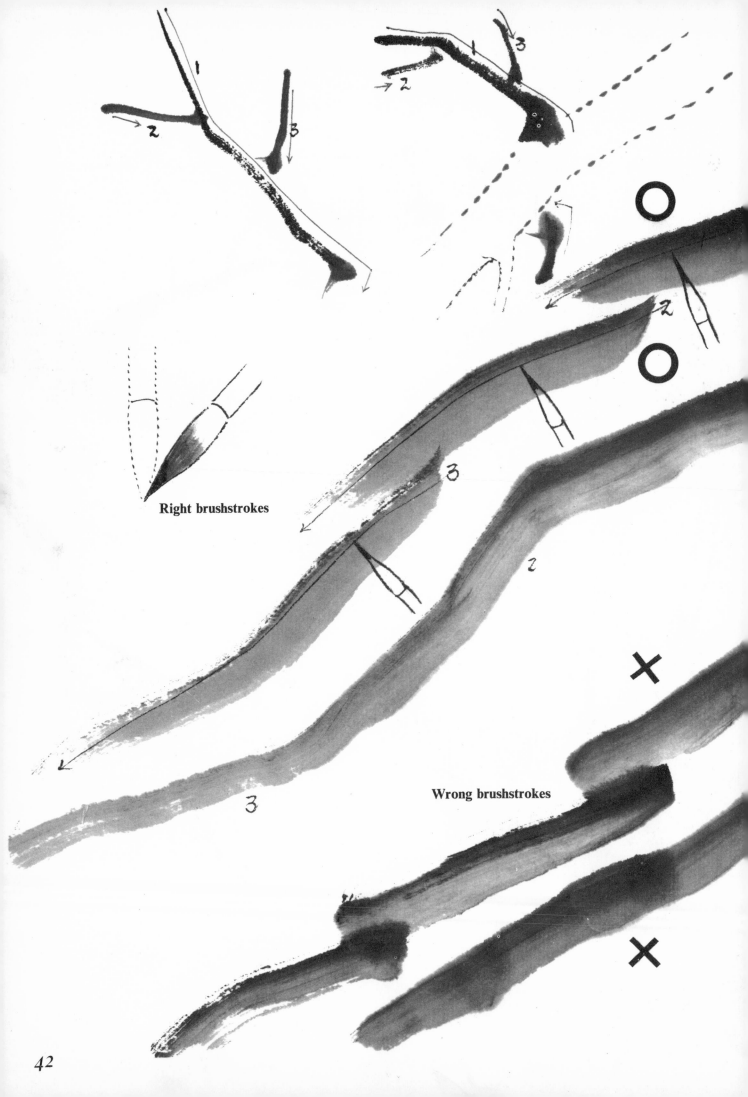

Right brushstrokes

Wrong brushstrokes

42

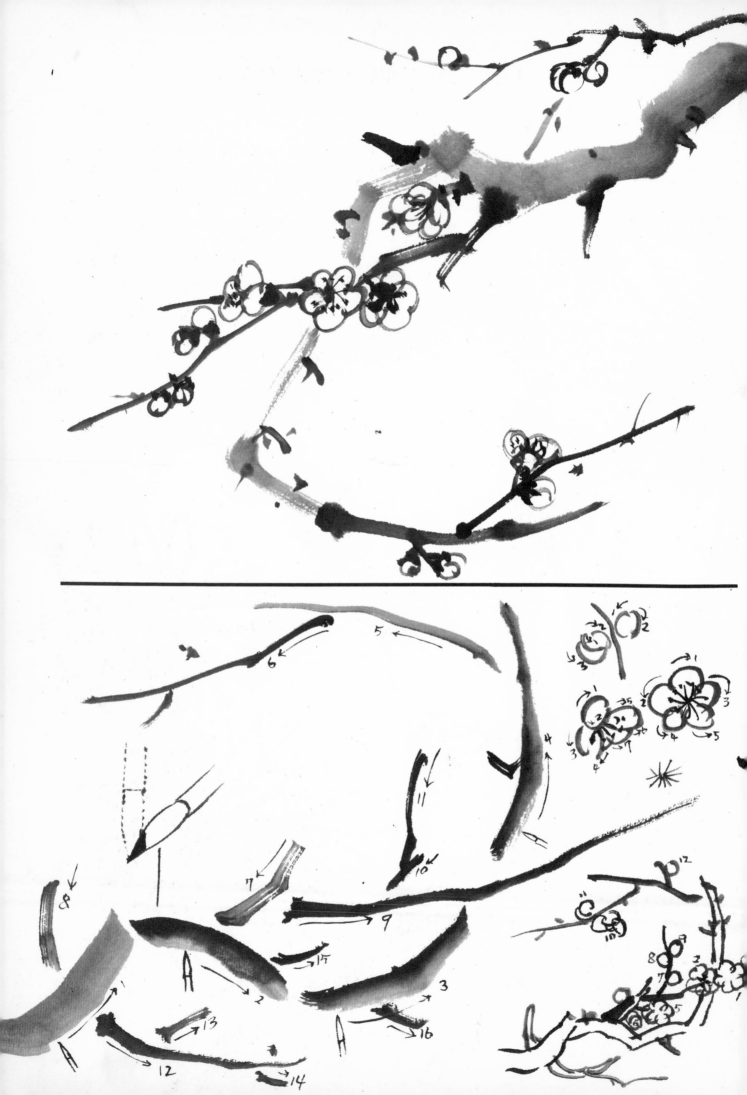

The Chrysanthemum

Flower

In painting the petals of the flower, use a two-toned brush (tanboku tipped with chuboku) and strive to make the shading as soft as possible. Paint all petals from the outside in—that is to say, toward the center.

Next, using a straight brush, paint the stem as shown in the accompanying diagram, varying the width of the strokes by increasing and decreasing the pressure on the brush. You must, of course, give the feeling that the heart and center of the flower rise directly from the stem.

Finally paint the leaves, once again following the direction of the arrows and using a side brushstroke. Once charged, a brush should have sufficient ink to paint two leaves.

tanboku

chuboku

noboku

47

A

B

C

The Pine Tree

Pine tree branches are similar to those of the plum, save that the smaller branches of the pine are curved where those of the plum are straight. Smaller branches, stemming from a larger one, are painted as the arrows in the accompanying diagram indicate.

After you have practiced, try to create your own variations using the basic stroke.

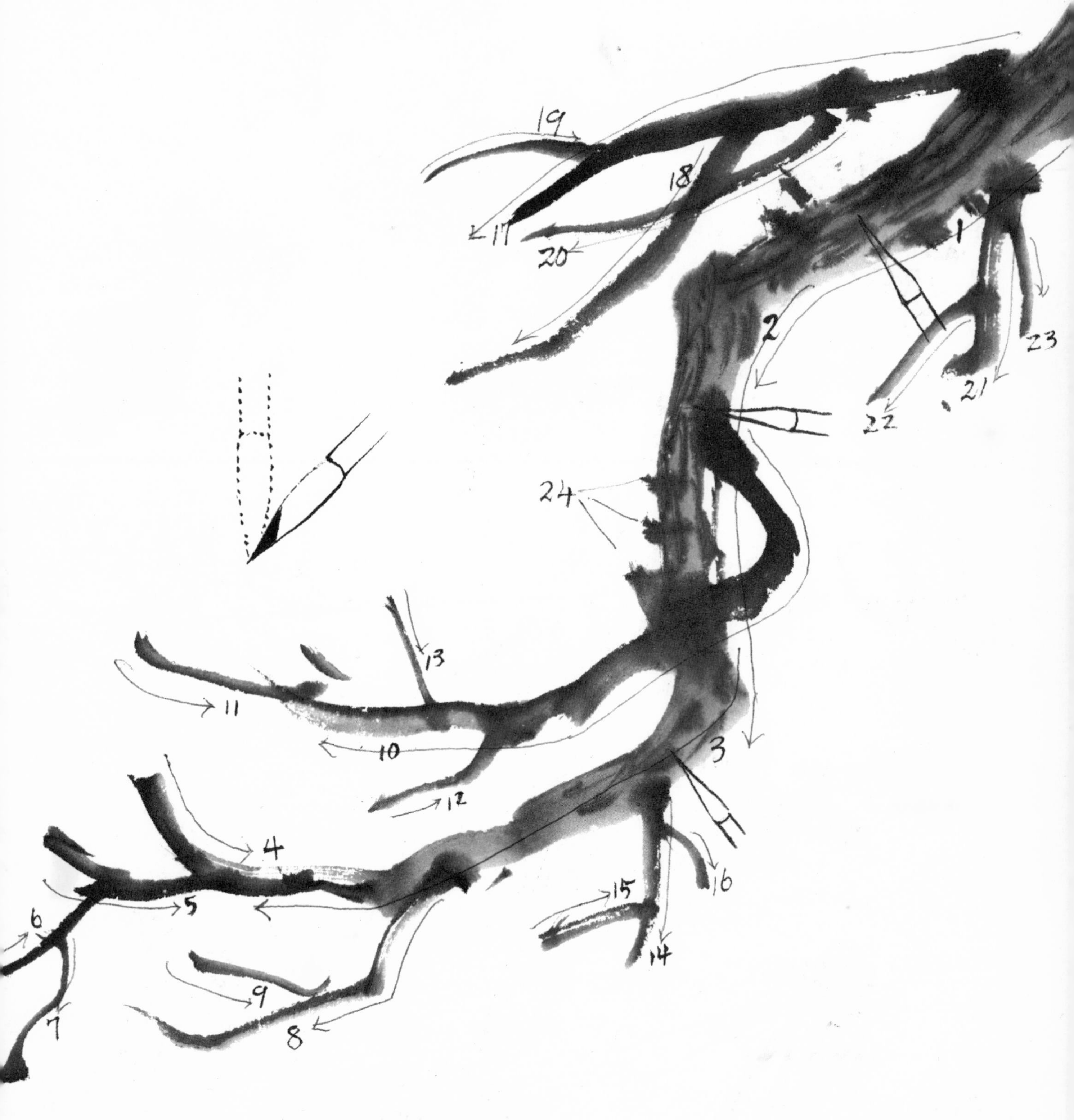

A. Paint the pine needles in pairs, keeping approximately the same distance between each pair of needles.

B. Begin at the point of the needle and widen it as it approaches the branch.

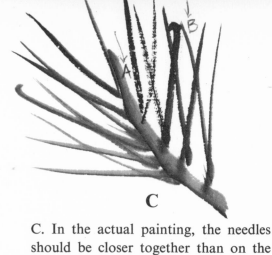

C. In the actual painting, the needles should be closer together than on the practice sheets.

D. This illustration, showing the needles at virtually a right angle to the branch, is given because it is an error common among beginning students.

Pine cones are painted with a side-brush, as shown.

While the ink of the tree trunk is still wet, paint in details of the bark.

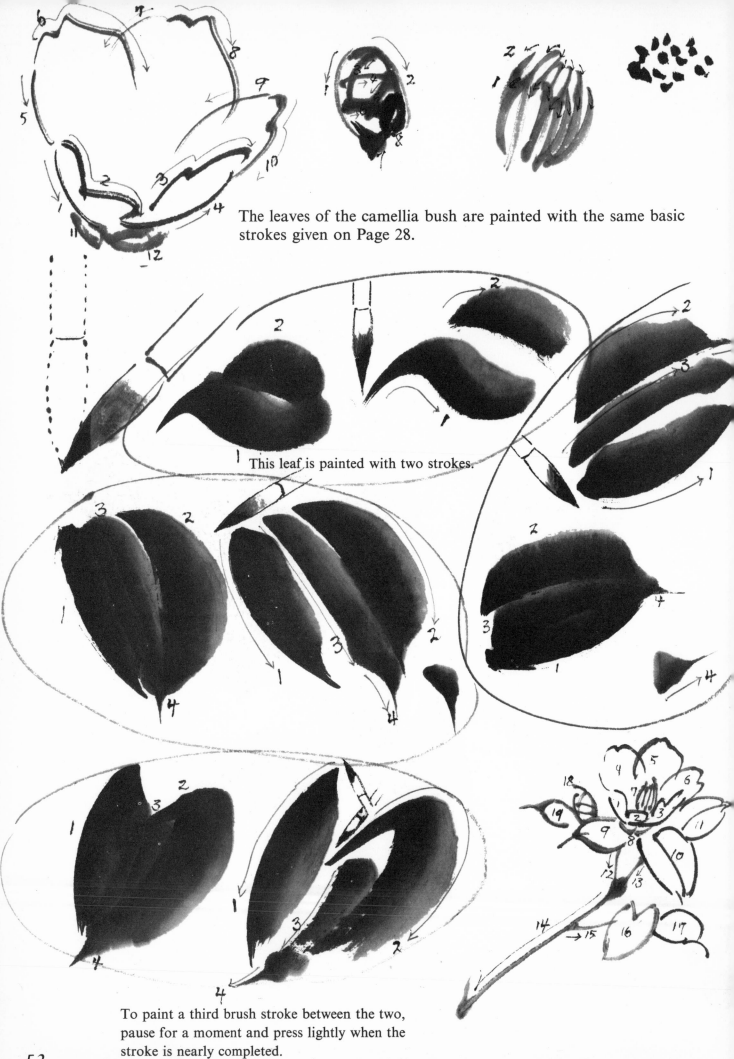

The leaves of the camellia bush are painted with the same basic strokes given on Page 28.

This leaf is painted with two strokes.

To paint a third brush stroke between the two, pause for a moment and press lightly when the stroke is nearly completed.

52

The Camellia

After charging brush with tanboku, re-move all excess water, pointing the brush firmly. Add noboku to the tip.

54

Pampas Grass with Bird

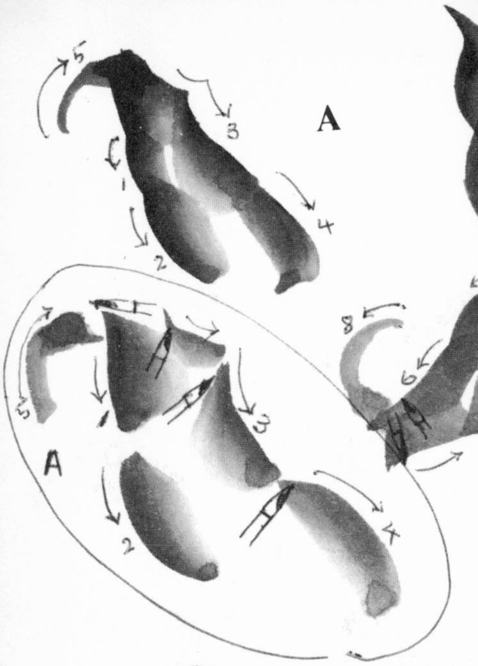

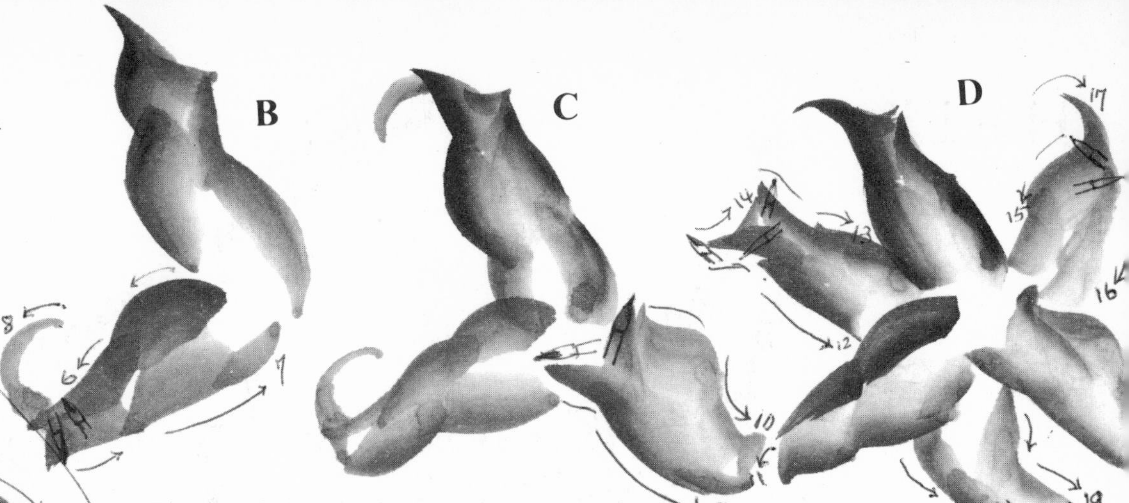

The brush handle is sometimes turned toward you, sometimes away from you, therefore follow the direction of the arrows in the accompanying diagram.

56

The Lily

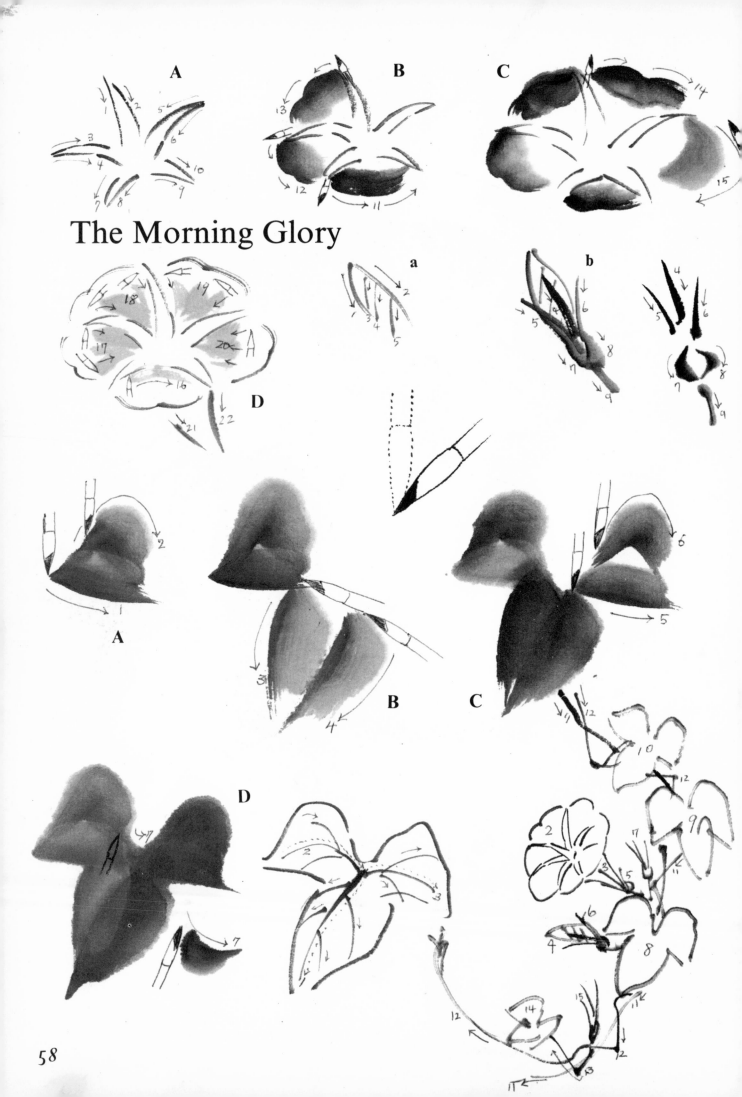

The Morning Glory

59

Persimmon with Bird

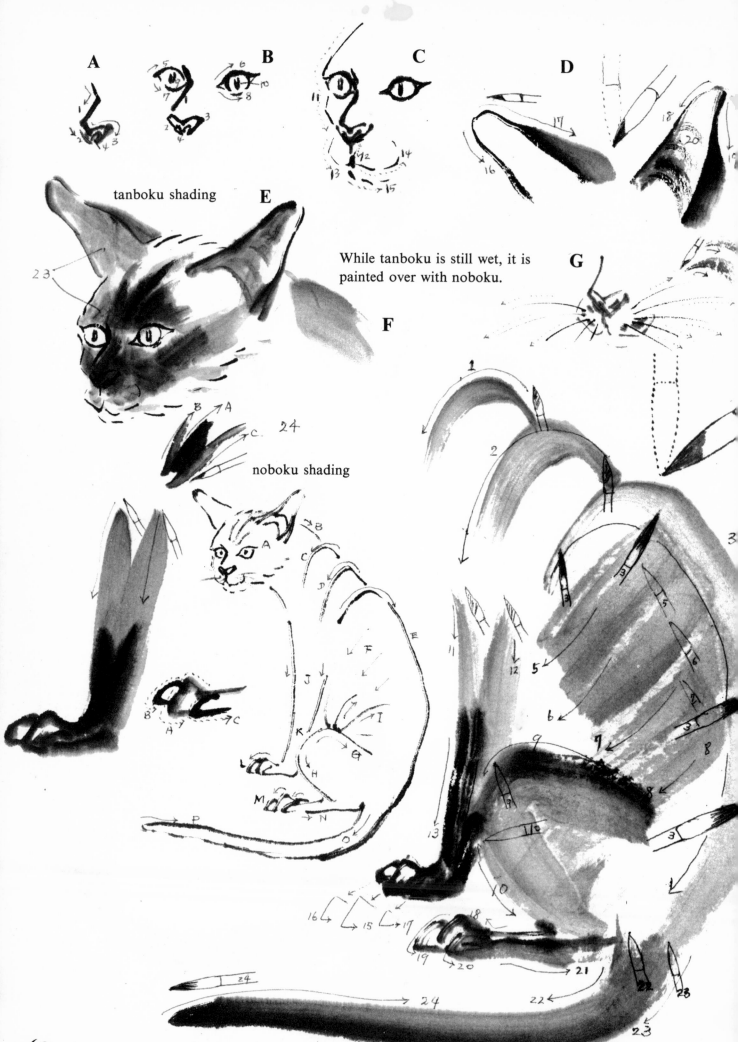

A B C D

tanboku shading

E

While tanboku is still wet, it is
painted over with noboku.

G

F

noboku shading

Cat

Monkey

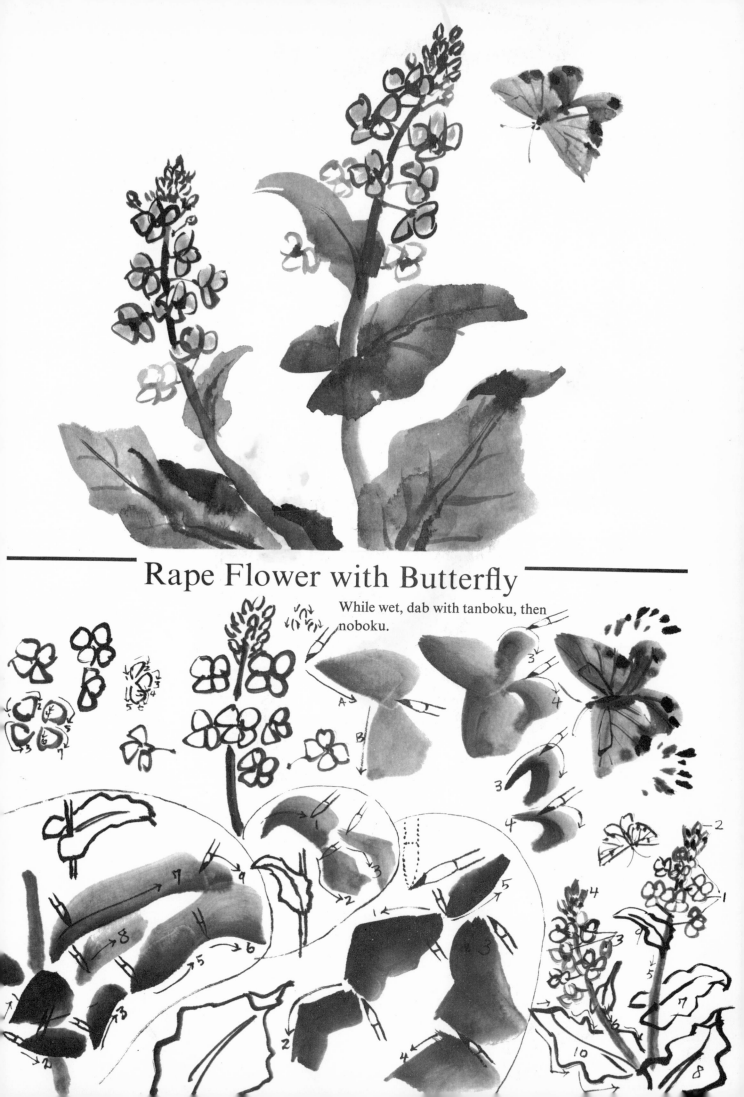

Rape Flower with Butterfly

While wet, dab with tanboku, then noboku.

Goldfish

The Maple Tree

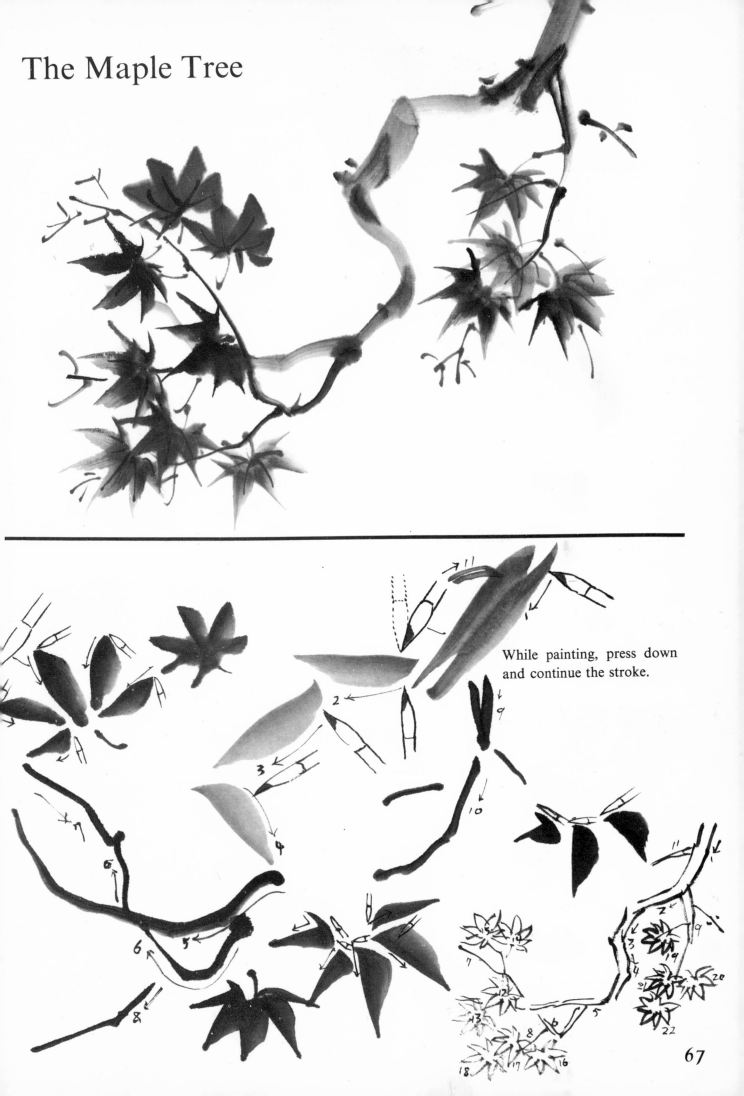

While painting, press down and continue the stroke.

Vegetables

68

After the Rain

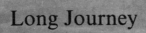

Long Journey

Moonlight

Boating

Landscape

Fishing Village

74

Fishing Village

75

Still Life

Wisteria with Bird

Rain

Landscape

Kanbei Oida

Applications

Now that you are acquainted with the fundamentals of sumi-e, many happy hours of ink-painting lie ahead of you—I hope! You must make your own compositions, of course, not confining

yourself to the kind of paintings given in the practice lessons. But
once having mastered them, you are ready to venture on your
own into the fascinating world of abstract ink-painting.

A

(A) Paint a gray line first, then a connecting black line.

B

(B) Paint a wide gray area, using one or more brushstrokes; then, while the gray is still wet, paint shapes into it with a dry brush.

C

(C) Paint a shape that pleases you with a dark brush; after the ink is dry, paint over it with gray.

D

(D) Take some object like a crushed sheet of paper, dip it in black ink, and make a print with it. After it is dry, wash over it with gray ink.

E

(E) Paint a gray area, and while it is still wet print a dark design over it, using the same sort of object, such as crushed paper, that you used in the preceding exercise.

F

(F) Using a wide brush, paint a gray area; then while it is still wet, trickle drops of gray ink over it.

G

(G) Superimpose a narrow dark line over a wider gray line; or try it the other way around —a narrow gray line with a wider dark line.

H

(H) Over a straight light line paint a narrower curved, dark line; or make the narrow curved line light and the wider straight line dark.

(I) Pour a bit of gray ink on the paper, then tilt it so that the ink flows freely, thus creating an agreeble and interesting line.

I